# New Organism
## Essais

*LETTER MACHINE EDITIONS*    *TUCSON, AZ*

# New Organism

**Essais**

Andrea Rexilius

Acknowledgments:

Thank you to the editors of the following journals for publishing versions of this work: *the Feminist Wire, Fanzine, The Bakery, Bombay Gin, Ampersand Review, Timber, Something on Paper, Jubilat, Evening Will Come, Trickhouse*, to Coconut Books for publishing an early version of *New Organism* as the chapbook, *Séance*, and to *Madame Harriette* for publishing a broadside of "I want to think like a magi."

"I want to think like a magi" was first published by the Academy of American Poets in 2013 for their Poem-a-Day series.

Thank you to HR Hegnauer for her writing on the word and, and to Tina Brown Celona, Mathias Svalina, Sommer Browning, Noah Eli Gordon, Joshua Marie Wilkinson, Olivia Cronk, and Julie Reid.

This book is dedicated to Eric Baus (the poet) and Virginia (the cat).

# *Contents*

## New Organism

## Essais

# NEW ORGANISM

# Séance

A Critical Theory of Grief Sensations

Secrecy can function as a group, to maintain the identity of that group. To maintain the group's shame. I have not yet functioned as a secret, as a person shrouded by shame. I have not been a group or the maintenance of a group. I have not seen a ghost, but I have dreamt one. I have not haunted anyone, but I have left traces in the hopes of haunting them. I have not built tunnels to the other side of anything. I have not collected or perused the undersides of tabletops, of slips, of bottoms of bottles, but oh, how I have wanted to come undone in this way. I have not come undone in many ways, having learned early on what the result is. I have at times lost touch with my body. I have felt more like an aura than an organism. I have feared being psychic. I have feared being seen by those who are psychic, of parenting an energy I could not control. I have short-circuited watches and radios involuntarily. I have not been present at a séance, but I have tried to conduct a séance.

A séance functions as perception. A stone feels like a dream. Imagine a dream with the weight of a stone or try in your dream to comb a stone. A stone breathes and a stone is reception traveling. I sleep with a stone in my ear. I listen to what the stone says. Is this a séance? A stone may hold some ghosts. I used to say a tree would be a good place for a ghost to live and that all allergies were the result of ghosts in the body. Put your body ghosts in trees and eat wheat again, eat nuts and milk and put your ghosts to rest. Take refuge in the newly revived heart, and stomach, and liver. There is no shame in loving a ghost, or in dreaming as a stone dreams, with shifty eyes, vessels cut open by the scalpel, a drowning man in flight beneath the water, like a body ghost loving a tree ghost loving a person.

Loving a person is a séance, in that it involves strangeness and necessity. It requires you to seize up in fits of possession. To become water, to become air, to become fluid. To say, *we are both horses again, aren't we. We are both in a race around this goddamn giant circle.* We are both heaving forward with all four hands on the floor. We are pressing down the floorboards with our tongues. Marking the points of erasure of a person. Licking up the stains the body leaves behind, swallowing their shadows in the morning. When I lean this close to the floorboards I hear the wood whispering. I hear myself whispering to the wood.

I hear myself whispering to the wood, at night, on hilltops. I hear myself whispering at night in my sleep. What are my eyelids saying. At night the room fluctuates. Climbs other rooms, other landscapes. I am steaming in this room while the other room heaves forward. Embeds itself in the coat rack and the doorframe, seeps in between pages of a book. Later I find traces of it. A residue on the countertop, a piece of bark in the sink drain. The impression of an ear on the wall. I have the distinct sense that the room is listening. The room is carving out new ideas beneath the skin. The pores soak in their salt, sweat out the room, move the room upward into the light. Let the room sink like a stone cradled inside the ear. The stone will absorb the room, not necessarily bring the room. Some people live on borrowed rooms and their eyes are shakier for it. It is best to dissolve a room like this, to walk away from it and not turn back to check its progress.

While this progresses I am bathed in sunlight drinking a glass of milk. I am lapping a glass of milk from a bowl in my undergarments like a cat. I look in the low places beneath the dresser, under the door. I put my paws beneath the door and meow. I press my body against the walls, against the books, against the chair legs. I press myself against the furniture and the clothes and the doorknobs. I press myself against the windows, and the screens, and the fabrics and ask plaintively why these things are here. What purpose does it serve to separate me from mountains and rivers, from ravines and roads and light of the sun and lampposts and stars. I look with my cat eyes at the scene outside the window. I watch dandelion fluff float by. I jump toward leaves I cannot reach. I howl at the other cats if they look at me. I howl and puff-up my tail in their direction. I spit and hiss at the doorframe. I try to escape but I no longer wish to escape.

I no longer wish to escape without a trace like rust under the red lights of the city. I no longer want to leave stones behind to find my way back to the house. I walk the cages of the street, rattling their abandonment. In the morning I stop at the post office. I walk through a glass door and suffer a migraine. I eat small vials of salt, and sand, and crushed oregano. I paint my ribcage red and make a print that looks like lungs on the wall. I reminisce about the color orange. I drink orange juice and lay on the lawn, still wet with dew. I watch clouds roll by and become a cloud. I sail into the air. I hyperventilate and come back down. I am a girl, and what does it feel like to be a girl. It feels like a hand over your mouth. A hand over your mouth and on your thighs. Some say it is the sound of a rabbit before it is caught. It is the sound of the sky before it comes crashing down.

Before it comes crashing down it is suspended. And then, as it moves, it evaporates. I conduct a study to find out which gender is more concerned with death. I find out it is men. I have never much regarded death, or cared one way or the other, as long as I do not die by the hands of men, in strange and brutal ways. Death has never been particularly interesting. I prefer the ocean depths or night sky to feel unwieldy. I have never wanted what was beyond death, except for the dust of it, to become a material. A fine grain of something. A thing the wind could truly lift. And to be disparate for once, and whole. To be in the sea and on the oak leaves. To be breath inside all the bodies and to be unseen and slipping through all of those hands, toward the light and away from the light, free of the face of the body.

I face my body when a moth faces light. I graze the edges of the room, edges of the city, edges of the continent. I touch water with my ankles and my fingertips. Weather moves and you move with it. Your pores unlatching, your thighs unhinged in wild grasses and flowers above the beach. Rushing headlong into them, them bending back and resting you gently against the earth. I told a girl I would meet her here, like this. We would know the moment. The sky would be a brand new sky. It would be bruised and clouds would rush toward us like smoke. We would make a pilgrimage then. We would live in the nest of grasses at the ocean. We would live in Sonoma County. It wouldn't matter when.

It wouldn't matter when the ice melted or when the fog lifted. It wouldn't matter how the water looked or where the horizon ended. We would not need a boat. I would become the boat or fin we would need to travel. I would become the face of death. I would face death and tell him to fuck off. I would tear up love letters death writes to me that are just Depeche Mode lyrics anyway. I will not drink Zima with death. I will not raise the roof with death. I walk away into a field of my own choosing, and as the sun comes down, I place the stone back inside my ear earnestly.

I place the stone back inside my ear earnestly. I swallow the world and I listen to the world. I have met the world's ghost. I am related to trees and I know the tree's ledge. I am related to trees and I used to be a tree. Now I am uprooted. I am a new organism craving light. My mother is Francesca Woodman. She is standing in a room with a turtle. Our great problem is post-revolutionary. A space where one can be a sensation and outplay the law. My mother, Francesca Woodman, is at a loss for words. She is unsayable. Her body is a body of pictures. Are these pictures shocking? Only if you are underwater. And then they reflect grief sensations.

Grief sensations touch the body the way light reverberates across water. The night of the ordeal of the grief one remembers the moon. Not the          . The moon was yellow. Tendrils. Clouds brushing the face. The sky not black but navy. The moon elongated. Harsh. Gloriously alive. Hot, sharp air against the face. The sky pressing the face. Thinking there is no difference, between what air is and what I am, except the pressure I put on it. The form I form around it. A critical theory of form. To breathe the word "air." To sculpt it invisible against the sky. To birth the moon from one's mouth. To birth a dark, heavy wound and heave it toward the sky. One born within you. One born upon you. Acted upon your body. Acted upon your birth. If light assaults the surface of your skin. No if light and not the skin shatters the way you face the moon in the sky.

If light shatters how you face the moon in the sky, it is important to say the word *stone*. To feel heavy in your belly the deep, brutal stone. The gallstone. The kidney stone. The many stones the body pockets as grief. The size of baseballs. The size of a tiny marble. The heat stone. The life stone. The brittle salt of the bone stone. To lick the enamel across your teeth. To bring to the surface that magma, that marrow, of the just beneath the skin stone.

I want to think like a magus—as stones underwater reflect grief. How images capture tone, and temperature of what is glimpsed. To glimpse why the root is made desperate by inability of its capture. Why, for instance, the word "woman" holds its own intention. One day on the street I found a fissure. I thought it was my sex. I thought it looked like the sea. An amoeba. I was not afraid to be seen. I was afraid to be dismembered. Do you see? The scene is one of red pooling into clear water. Men want to see you bleed, my mother said. Like a gutted fish, she said. Like a submerged memory. On the surface of the water I see an article. Perhaps the nuance is unintentional. Is it a verb? Is it a noun? The way female bodies surface. But I like the way a woman looks possessed, like a new organism under water.

"We must move on to the rhetoric of women, one that is anchored in the organism, in the body" (Duras). Pushed back by the flood of a veiled history. The earth. A monotonous violence. The error.  For we have not learned a thing. The pulse of testimony a vow to dream the intention. The pulse of testimony no longer requires illumination. It is illuminating this polished shore to hopefulness. Witness here, and answer. What is the female body's landscape? What is the rhetoric of her landscape? A shore. A margin. Coral reef. A rift. A fault. Yes, a faultline. Where land meets shore. A divide occurs. Where continent advances and deposits its silt. A slit in the I. The essence of an enemy felled. It is not a matter of passion. Storms, impoverishments already revealed in Scripture. It is to split the body of the body. As if it were a condition.

The act of adoration as a condition. An expanse. The water opening a window. Bottomless pain at the juncture. The act of transport a very likely condition. Retelling, in every instance, what prevailed. I am unable to detail a personal history. Merely gesture toward air that circulates around the crux of it. That there was nature—murky water, dirt—seems important. I do not wish to tell. Not to expose, but to create exposure. I take photographs of water underneath the water and the photographs are ruined. I have nothing left to say and I am not saying it now. These are the repercussions of language.

The repercussions of language taste stones. Dream stones that have been inside the ears. Body stones that have been inside the gallbladder, the silt of the liver. To know truly what a sediment is. To know it is residue, but not of the land. Of a sentiment. An emotional field. The place where wildflowers bend in the wind. The place where perspiration becomes precipitation. I balance stones on a precipice. My body lunges and heaves, pulled by the tide.

They say if you are a woman you are pulled by the tide. They call you a lunatic, hysterical because the moon, full, makes you bleed. They suggest a hysterectomy. They suggest you stop troubling yourself with a vote. There is no need for a voice when you have an animal between your legs.

The animal that is my sex is not a novel. This is a novel. This caused a rhizomatic membrane. I am faltering here. In the white snow of the white page. Yesterday I watched a Tarkovsky film in Russian. The translation was "look how peculiar the sky. The sky." I meandered back inside the doorway just as it began to pour. All of the grain in the field writhing. I struck the yellow leaves with my fist. I struck the grey sky and the mud beneath my feet. I don't know what being human means. Is it to have eyes? Here is the ground, the field. The air around me a room. A room that pulses and heaves. The light, clear. The light, not yellow. My breath, not yellow or clear. The words, leaves upon my breath. The turning of the seasons fall off of my mouth. My mouth lingers. The sun sets. Some animal burrows its dark fur inside this sentence.

This sentence is mercurial. The point you see at the end is the finest tip of a flame. And now Walden is on fire. And now Walden is wet with moss growing on it. And the roots of a narrative bloom and curl under what Walden is. Where there is stitch there is also under stitch. We ask how do I mark how this sings? This blank note in the throat which resonates. Phantasmagoria. The uvula. All uvula.

All uvula shall come to pass. Shall come to parable shall come to prosper. Come what may. Come what will. All shall come to be blinded and bound. With faith. With a lack of passion. With a lack of lingering embrace. All shall come forward and crawl through the gates of heaven through the gates of hell. All shall come to pass William Blake on the road having visions. All are born again. This world. This wound keeps moving.

All this wound keeps moving, Anna Karenina. In theory Anna Karenina is my mother. But this is a dark place to be. Forgotten. Splitting the valve of the space-time continuum. What is that face in the sky? It is a child's face. Go on.

I blink and the film has changed. No longer Russian, or Lithuanian, but French. *À naitre de la Prairie. Né de l'incendie. El Venado sur la langue.* To be born is a poor station. And, oh, how it aches inside the tongue. Here is a world of flesh. Here a prairie. Ground rises out of me. Mechanism. The social meaning of *Girl.* Assembling something perpetual. I am transcribing the contemporary. I weep then at facts and am amazed.

Wrong. You need to understand. And I need to under-
stand in the future. To lay that territory open. I would
have. And I'm going to need to. Be wrong in America.
Even in terms of the future. And I'm going to need to
imagine what it could be yet it's still in rational terms, for
the most part. To lay that territory open. Let me ask a
few things and say a few things wrongly. Like the totality
I would have in order to understand a specific instance.
It seemed to me I was so domineering when really I was
just a girl in a specific instance of action. Lifting an arm
to ask a semi-polite question. Lifting an arm to pull the
emergency cord. To say. To Séance.

# First Residue

Perforation

*What is the relationship between the text and the body*
*in your writing?*

A conclusion of nothing. The constructing tongue makes
it possible to want. I prefer to start in this place. Between
a rabbit and a duck. Between a situation of withholding.
I have symptoms. I set out to eliminate them. But this
has the unfortunate tendency of instrument, which has at
least three roles here: dissemination, silhouette, tableau.
Connectivity creates a plane that makes this possible.
An interruption in a field of immanence. I take this field
to be, among other things, a limitation. A situation of
beholding my role in psychic and social life. There are
clearly other reasons.

*What is the relationship between the text and the body in your writing?*

The text refuses bandages. It wants its own unexplained presence. Its own gender trouble. Its own regard for the pain of others. Its own awe. Its own words that wound. Its own craft of research. Its own looking. Its own notes from no man's land. Its own styles of radical will. Its own vertical interrogation. Its own pedagogy of the oppressed.

*What is the relationship between the text and the body in your writing?*

What is relationship? Departure. Ecstatic shattering. Unbinding. A sounding into the realm of the leap. Conduction. Apprehension. Transition.

*What is the relationship between the text and the body in your writing?*

It sees a woman's body. An escalating, asymptotic body. An incoherent body. A libidinal body. A regime of female attractiveness. A manifold body. A body that marks the course of human history. A deployed body. A sexually assaulted body that refuses. A body that accuses. A constant locus of resistance to pain, or constriction, or tedium, or semi self-starvation, or condemnation. A rebellion. This body embarks because it is necessary. Though impulse alone is not inevitable. This body holds no preoccupation with youth or beauty. It holds no orientation to "styles of the flesh."

*What is the relationship between the text and the body in your writing?*

In the open without a definite territory or identity, I am ignorant of my own way of filling in a gap. I remain an awkward, dancing, terrorist figure, and denounce it. And pronounce it. It has established a permanent state of emergency. The question is, Why not see a discipline as an organ for perceiving light?

# Second Residue

The Woods

All girls have religious experiences. It is what makes them human. As we have seen girls use culturally mandated appearance norms to achieve their personal ends. They are not unlike an animal rising out of the ground.

A girl rises out of the ground carrying roots in her mouth.
I rise out of the ground carrying roots in my mouth.

Out of the ground toward lyric openness.
Becoming a less limited self.
Becoming a subject in language. More than
just a beat or signature of yourself in multiple. I am
trying to find un-endangered sites. Field
or depth of self. Description as a way of erasing
delineation. Here a blue shock of air. Becoming
weathered. Here a flock de-contextualized. We
were impatient and ridiculous. Never
more drastic than managing to end the sentence
in a bright black void.

A girl rises out of the woods carrying the woods in her mouth.
I rise out of the woods carrying the woods in my mouth.

To mouth the word *woman*,

something of a phantom,

oscillating between the not yet

and the no longer.

Out in the world she goes again

 to remind herself to take up less space.

"I had left in order to starve."

To achieve the sick wisdom

of the mandatory.

But what if I get pregnant.

What if they break all of my bones.

To escape in form.

To escape as my own country.


                    To escape as my own resident.

          Raymond Ledrut observes, "The city [woman]

                is not an object produced by a group

in order to be bought or even used by others. The city

[woman] is an environment formed by the interaction

              and integration of different practices.

     It is maybe in this way that the city [woman] is truly

                      the city [woman]."

Just as territory retains its own narrative pressure.

Just as territory is discourse.

She wakes up and is Antarctica.

She wakes up and is transcribed.

A territory is not a blank page.

It is the book buried beneath the ground.

The historical ground moving underfoot.

The territory as a changing field appears to be a local story.

I can only hint at however strange in appearance

or obscure in origin she is.


The woman leaves the ground carrying a rhizome in her mouth.

      I leave the ground carrying a rhizome in my mouth.


There is a joke here about the woman with the rhizome in
her mouth. No. Not that kind of rhizome. And you, male
reader, should meet my gaze and be ashamed.

# To Be A Human Is To Be A

"I" has no story of its own

What emerges is learning to construct

Residue

What it propels

What it insinuates

Narrative is not so forlorn

Unlikable


No, to tell a story is gene-encoded

The mythos of human address

Abandoned

since before the void

formation reconstruction

Deranged agency but rather that than an object of

speech


Discontinuous residence of story

Aperture in the holding space

Fixture/life of erogenous zones

With the body as a starting point

External impulses

Touched/moved from within

I wake up in this haze of violence. To be human is to go to war. Don't look at me. I will blow up your genitals. You are unrecognizable to my own face in the mirror. Even though you are flesh-like and pure. Here, cover your body in this drape. Dig a hole and go to sleep there.

With the body as a starting point
To embalm
To make use of
And for reassurance
To preoccupy
That site of construction

There is blood. There is heat here. And I want to liberate my skin. Sometimes when you move I see your skeleton and remember. It is animal you inhabit.

I heard a scream
At night
In the morning
Found
Fresh rabbit

Skin in the chain link

Of the fence


I am going to suffer. My tongue has never touched the body of our lord. It remains cloaked. Expert at reading other textures.


A narrative contains the following:

Censure

Caesura

Seizure

A narrative ducks and covers.

1. There is loss.
2. There is directive.
3. There is failed attempt.


To embrace. One hand holds mechanism. To make new organism. Place it above your head. Hold toward the sky. Terror. Electrocution. No, this is the wrong organism. Repulsion.

Revolution

Is a tame verb

In the 21<sup>st</sup> century

Not the civic model

It used to be

when things truly revolved

when we dug up the death

of those bodies, and put them

back together.

Hold the tarot card in your hand up to the light. Is it the
fool, or the wheel of fortune?

the female rhizome

The lyric lately is parenthetical.

Let us examine the residuum.

Of conjunctive.

Of repetition and difference.

Nonetheless the female animal invited experimentation.

She has yet to speak, to advance a different spectrum of identity.

One that does not have to do with genitals, or genre.

The woman cannot organize her desires.

Her critical distance is that she is spectacle.

That she passes for social discourse.

But is embodied in a poetry that will not shun spectacle.

For instance, she is not affiliated with literariness or gravity.

Her poetry may objectify this sort of philosophy.

Keeping the woman dead.

For her, aggression cannot be a radical poetics.

The aggressive woman is not considered radical.

It is only by running your fingers though pubic hair and inserting

the mirror that your desires open within these fixed margins.

The annotated "here" was written under fixed conditions.

The woman, as I have noted above, is a meta-poetic lyric.

"Here" is a woman.

Wait.

Where is she?

She is on the page.

She is standing in front of you.

She is transcribing this shaking fist at your partition.

Yes, the woman is vast, enormous, incalculable really.

She was so tall, so big, her presence so huge

she couldn't help having an aesthetic influence.

To expand orientation in ways not thought possible.

When you have chosen a word to influence.

To reflect the nuance of translation,

translate it into a language older than English.

It is basically made out of her bodies.

The "here" could be more abstract.

An experience operating on a human and geological scale.

An anatomy of rupture.

It is basically made out of cross-sections.

The basic utility of how things come together.

It is hard to tell if a woman is floating or levitating.

I would like to see her autonomy more clearly, as a roadmap.

As a sonnet.

The indentations I am talking about are on her, as a city.

Periods. End-stopped lines.

Epigraphs. The conjunction.

Society writes her organic in urban settings.

Society writes her desire, fucking, end-stopped, overflowing.

Her city as a system of time passing.

Autobiographical. Alchemical.

The world obsesses and blurs the distinction.

The lofty interiors of the woman.

Those books she writes with her bodies.

Her animal open on a stage.

Perhaps to stain her. To collapse some distance. To colonize.

To reach inside and pull her intestines out. To break her jawbone.

To break her mouth. To murder and rape—her female children.

To slice her clitoris off. To remove her breasts.

Describing these /her "landscapes" we wean on them
　　and are pervaded.

Although the poems realize this encounter.

These sites of gathering, a hyphen.

These habitats at sea.

The entire assaulted continent hazarded.

Itself a sense of resisting.

Her indigenous shell-mounds speak.

I find this place of passage utterly foreign.

The trespass of deep proximity.

To birth. To bear within your flesh the flesh of another.

And to be treated like you are a heretic.

And to be treated like you are a whore.

And to be treated like a beach-front property.

White is purity, etc.

Of course, one sees what one wants to see.

Enough to be haunted by the language-object.

The kinetic subliminal collapse.

I have the sense that I can create a place.

I have a sense that language transmits multiple signals.

Though the strata I see is not entirely drawn to the line.

The sentence itself incapable of the impossible.

And at the expense of failing the movement.

It unfolds its ribs against our predigested air.

In light of this national crisis.

What am I speaking of?

The wound.

Where is it located.

On the psyche.

On her sex.

There are some real demons in the distance.

Her vulnerability.

Her vulva in which one may wedge a foot.

The door.

The beak.

The territory.

To speak as I believe the whites of the eye speak.

And to see as the space between is danger.

And to say as the multiple is the danger.

The approach— still only an image.

Our imaginary landscape of the word "woman."

It is not silent but speaks as absence.

It speaks, but without any beginning.

# ESSAIS

# Root Systems of Narrative

A Séance

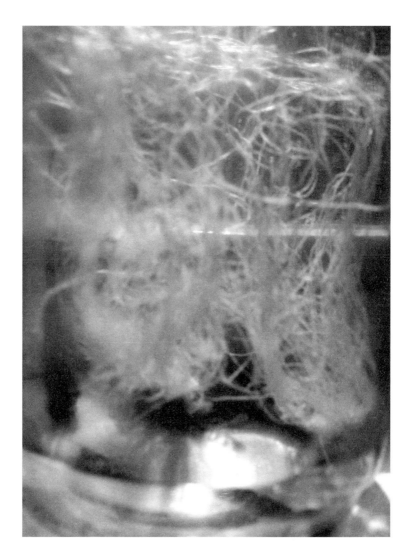

I like rusted textures, knots, tangled lines, elbows, crosshairs, weathering. I have been gathering things for a long time. When I was a child we lived near a railroad track and a river. I gathered railroad spikes. I remember looking for the discolored ones. The ones with spots of oil or scratches or paint on them. I didn't like the solid ones or the new ones. I put them in a bucket on the front porch next to an aquarium of tadpoles from the river. I like machinery and organism. I look for both separately or simultaneously in my narrative.

I tend to gather alike things in language. I obsess over an idea or a term or an image and use it over and over again in a variety of contexts. Images are cumulative or regenerative. They have to be allowed to exist in almost every context before we can pretend to know anything about them. I find I have to use my body in order to write well. I go for a walk first and gather things and pretend to be a diorama. Then words conduct themselves. If I don't go for a walk first, I gather things from books. I move through books the same way I move through walks. I turn to pages and find the field jar. Then I put all of the field jar elements onto a page. Then I cut and paste them. I have to trust my first instinct or there is a massacre. I have tried many times to undo a massacre. Everyone knows things are hacked up and put back together when that happens. They sense a murder has occurred and are uncomfortable.

I find things when the shift occurs, when it doesn't I am just going for a walk. I know the shift when I begin to see the world as more colorful. It is sort of like the difference between visiting a place and living in it. Sometimes you are at a remove from a landscape, just moving through it, looking at it. Other times it permeates you. You are more like a child in it. I am never actively "looking" for things. I am observing and waiting for them to show up. I am finding something that looks like it has been placed there, like it is also waiting for me to notice it. It is also about detail. About finding something small, something that gathers its own weight when you lift it out of context. This is the difference between "good" narrative and "garbage." If you pick something up and it looks like garbage when you are holding it, it probably is garbage. If it looks like something else, something in addition to what it looked like on the ground, it is narrative.

A field jar is a collection or an installation of the day's findings. On certain walks I'll notice I'm finding the same shades of green or yellow again and again. These colors begin to be what I am waiting for. I walk around and many of them show up on the path I chose. I put them in my pocket. As soon as I get home I put them, in the order they are removed from my pocket, into a mason jar. I don't arrange them. I drop them in and allow them to arrange themselves. Whenever I have tried to arrange them, they begin to resemble "trash" instead of "narrative." They have to assemble themselves.

I point to the ground a lot. This is a way of recognizing where things are without touching them. The things that are pointed to usually cannot be picked up. They are shadows or circumstances, or ground installations. Things that would not fit in a pocket or that are wet or slimy or too cumbersome to carry. They are also things that are only good in context. If they were lifted out something would be lost. The grass or dirt or water or whatever texture or color surrounds them must also remain. I am very good at holding still, both on the inside and the outside. I practiced meditating by staring at the radiator when I was a child. There is a recording of me (a sound recording) where my mother is saying my name over and over and I don't answer. I don't seem to hear her. Finally she comes into the room. She sees me and says in a very quiet, concerned voice, "What are you doing?" I make a small sound, a breath with a vowel attached. She seems annoyed and says, "Dinner is ready." For some reason I can hear that recording and remember what I was doing. I would sit in front of the radiator and stare at its legs until the legs moved away from themselves and toward me. That is kind of what I am doing when I look for narrative. I am holding still and waiting for things to move toward me.

Most of the things related to narrative gathering are things that I knew growing up. Both of my grandfathers lived on farms in Southern Illinois. I went for walks at both of their houses and gathered things. I gathered organic things and metallic things. My father is another gatherer. We had a garage full of rusty nails, old bicycle seats with coils that looked like nests, bicycle wheels, large red cabinets full of washers, and screws and wire. He kept rocks, and shells, and paintbrushes. He kept old piano parts. At some point we had just the inside of a piano, a large frame of wood with strings on it and a shelf with the keys. You played it by plucking the exposed strings. He also collected old books, encyclopedias, field guides, books about celestial objects, books about other cultures, books about languages. These things were never particularly present in our family life. My father never talked about these things or why he was attracted to them. Sometimes I suspect he was only attracted to them because I needed to find them. The garage was like a museum. I would spend hours tunneling through it. Gathering things, building nests to hide in, reading things, making sculptures. We also had a victrola. I don't think it was ever played while I was growing up, but I have it now. The shape of its cabinet and its arm are familiar to me. The sound it makes is the sound of the objects inside the garage. It is them if they were music. I think that many of my memories are composed of these objects, so I often dream about them.

# "I"

the lyric self as rhizome

## Entryway I: Definition

When I write a new poem, the main question I face is a question of pronouns. Not who is the "they" here or who is the "you" here, but who is the "I" here. It is not an issue of self-identity but an issue of fracture or consistency. I begin to wonder how the "I" will travel. Will "I" maintain a similar perspective throughout a manuscript articulated by this "I"? Will "I" represent shifting points of view, locations, times, states of consciousness, states of being? Will "I" always be me, from my perspective, or will "I" sometimes play the parts of others? Will "I" become something other than "I" was at the start, or will "I" remain the same? Whitman's famous lines come to mind here: "Do I contradict myself? / Very well, then I contradict myself, (I am large. I contain multitudes.)" In some ways this answers it and ends my essay before it even begins, but where Whitman contains multitudes (I picture layer upon layer of self), I'm interested perhaps not in contradiction but in interruption, in starting and pausing, beginning, becoming: as a necessary and symptomatic dimension of the lyric and, more particularly, of the lyric self.

I am interested in the rhizome as an autonomous concept, as a term not entirely tied to the theories of Giles Deleuze and Felix Guattari, as a term that might rupture (i.e., engage) those entryways, as a term that enacts that which it names, in other words, a rhizomatic definition of the rhizome as it is related to the lyric self. For a few years now, I've been thinking about the etymology of the word "and." "And" is a rhizomatic word, a word that accumulates, that mimics the motion of becoming, that gestures toward new entryways, additions, a word that builds, not unlike the Winchester house, onto the body of a sentence. "And" is an alchemical word. It begins in our DNA. It winds around us. It stutters forward and haunts our bodies, our edges, our permutations. If I have a poetics, it is related to the word "and." And if I have a lyric speaker, I would rather she be called "and" than "I."

Gertrude Stein…in her *Composition as Explanation* [talks about] beginning again and again. Truth is not something that can be uncovered; it can only be rediscovered, day after day. The value of breaking through the dead rubble each morning and in viewing each object from as many angles as possible is that one keeps one's mind open, that conclusions are always tentative and that the process of discovery is always more important than any particular end result.[1]

This is the nature of "and." The nature of "I" is less becoming. "I" is a capitalization, an outsider, an observer. "And" participates. In *A Thousand Plateaus*, Deleuze and Guattari also mention the word "and." They write, "The tree imposes the verb 'to be,' but the fabric of the rhizome is the conjunction, and...and... and..."[2] This conjunction carries enough force to shake and uproot the verb "to be." The lyric "and," then, is not about being but about shaking up and uprooting. It is about perpetual becoming.

## Entryway II: The Essay

*Essayer* is the French verb meaning 'to try' and an *essai*
is an attempt.

—O.E.D.

"The essayist gives you his thoughts, and lets you know,
in addition, how he came by them."

—Alexander Smith[3]

"The essay is an enactment of the creation of the self."

—Philip Lopate[4]

"The usual reproach against the essay, that it is frag-
mentary and random, itself assumes the givenness of
totality and…suggests that man is in control of totality.
But the desire of the essay is not to seek and filter the
eternal out of the transitory; it wants, rather, to make the
transitory eternal."

—Theodor Adorno[5]

"The practice of experimenting, or trying something out, is expressed in the now uncommon sense of the verb *to prove*—the sense of 'testing' rather than of 'demonstrating validity.' Montaigne 'proved' his ideas in that he tried them out in his essays. He spun out their implications, sampled their suggestions. He did not argue or try to persuade. He had no investment in winning over his audience to his opinion; accordingly, he had no fear of being refuted. On the contrary, he expected that some of the ideas he expressed would change, as they did in later essays. Refutation represented not a personal defeat but an advance toward truth as valuable as confirmation. To 'prove' an idea, for Montaigne, was to examine it in order to *find out* how true it was."

—William Zeiger[6]

## Entryway III: Attempting Embrace

In the essay, the attempt is in the idea. In the lyric, the attempt (reach, embrace, desire, etc.) is toward the self, toward the ever-absent and ever-present speaker "I." The other day I was talking to a friend about exile and diaspora and why I am drawn to literature that explores these concepts. What could I possibly know about exile or diaspora? From what have I been exiled? From what have I been shattered out of, if not my self, my form, my body, my sight? All linguistic engagement attempts to carve out this form, to give it shape, to give it genre. The lyric speaker pivots on this exact dilemma, to both be the self and not be the self simultaneously, to speak not as "I" but as "and." The word "residence" and, from within this word, the word "residue" enact this for me. The lyric "I" is a residence, but it is a residence that is visible or conceptual only as residue. Residue, to distinguish from trace, leaves a stain or an echo of itself. The residue of a cup of coffee does not look like a cup of coffee, but it signals this larger residence of the cup. This is not to say that the stain becomes the cup, but that the stain marks a simultaneous presence and absence in residence.

In *Lyric Poetry: The Pain and Pleasure of Words*, Mutlu Blasing writes extensively about the nature of the "I" in lyric poetry. He notes that "The gap that the 'I' occupies is the internal gap of language, and it is also the site that the reader must occupy."[7] And in *The New Princeton Encyclopedia of Poetry and Poetics*, we find that "The speaker is a device for making the invisible visible. Paul de Man replaces such standard terms as 'personification' with 'catachresis' in order to explain the function of the frequent trope of address in lyric poetry. The poet-surrogate is replaced by the figurative voice, a mantic or shamanistic presence that makes the verbal world of the lyric a visible world to the mind of the reader."[8] "I" is destabilized or rhizomatic in a number of ways. "I" is myself *and* reader *and* gap *and* surrogate *and* site *and* device.

Additionally "I," as we have seen, is not really "I" (as in me, myself). "I" is something larger, something projected, inhabited by something other than "I." "I" is also they and he and we. Blasing would say that the I in poetry is both the generic "I" of language and an individuated "I" sounded by the materials of language. Paul de Man argues that "the principle of intelligibility, in lyric poetry, depends on the phenomenalization of the poetic voice (which is) the aesthetic presence that determines the hermeneutics of the I."[9] And Jonathan Culler declares that "the fundamental aspect of lyric writing...is to produce an apparently phenomenal world through the figure of voice."[10] "I" is an appearance of a disappeared self. Like the planchette, the voice of the lyric speaker is a tongue that empties itself and allows for multiple inhabitants. As Rimbaud says, I is another. And another and another and another.

## Entryway IV: Cindy Sherman

Cindy Sherman's "self-portraits" have always fascinated me. I've used her work, alongside Frida Kahlo's self-portraits, to introduce composition classes to the personal essay. I use Sherman and Kahlo as examples of destabilizing the "I" while also rendering it as fully intact, as witness and witnessed. The idea that one is both seeing and being seen by oneself is important. Transformation can only take place in this intermediary space of destabilized self-location. The best writing comes out of this kind of exile. This is also true for the lyric, in which the creation of the self as in the essay is marked and marred by the authorial "I." Frida Kahlo and Cindy Sherman represent a visual example of what this marring might look like, how it might manifest from poem to poem, from book to book, or from I to I.

Adorno writes that "the desire of the essay is not to seek and filter the eternal out of the transitory; it wants, rather, to make the transitory eternal." Kahlo's and especially Sherman's images are this transitory made eternal. My main goal in writing is to transcend this notion of the "I," to speak from an experience larger than the confines of my own physical body and all that my physical body has seen, endured, and enacted. In an interview in *What is Poetry?*, Lewis Warsh notes that "Identity is often slippery, and the way I write is only synonymous with who I am at the moment."[11] This is true, but I want something even larger than multiple perspectives. I want to speak from multiple bodies, whatever that entails. Michael Palmer says, "I'm not sure I've ever actually met the author. The author passes through my life, a kind of presence-absence, but we do not speak."[12] I like this idea a little better. The author becomes a kind of shadow self. There is an intersection, a crossroads by which we pass through one another, but we do not merge.

Cindy Sherman's "self-portraits" also convey a presence-absence. There are a number of essays written about the insignificance of her using her own body to create these photographs. They are said to not comment on identity. For me, though, and I think for many others, the most interesting thing about these photos is the simultaneous presence and absence of Cindy Sherman. Or as Harryette Mullen says, "I don't know if I'm undermining identity so much as continually rewriting and revising it."[13] This acknowledgment of a very basic instability, of the eternal transience of "I" is the face of a lyric self as rhizome.

## Entryway V: Revision

Kurt Schwitters' Merzbau,[14] Madeline Gins and Arakawa's architectural bodies that attempt to make dying illegal,[15] and the Winchester House[16] haunt me. "…The fabric of the rhizome is the conjunction, 'and…and…and…'" In one definition "and" accumulates, begins again and again, is in a state of perpetual becoming. "And" moves away from linear narratives that might confine us to a paradigm of life and death, and saves us from ghosts that will stalk and murder us if we don't continue to adapt. "And" is a bodily extension, a physical manifestation of externalized nest, a pathway. "And" desires the rupture of addition. "And" is a manifesto.

And to move away from just this idea of accumulation, I've noticed recently my shift in love from Georges Perec to Francis Ponge. No longer is the list of objects, the list of accumulation enough. I want metaphorical metamorphosis. Not just the list, but a reading (interpretation) of that list. If I am going to be haunted, I want a séance. I want to be included as an active participant, not a collector, but a diviner. In fact, part of what draws me to Schwitters, Gins and Arakawa, Ponge, and the Winchester house is their spine-tingling alchemy. The strangeness of their inevitable necessity.

This desire to be not a collector but a diviner strikes me as being tied to Levinas's terms the *saying* and the *said*. He writes, "The saying in poetry, interwoven in poetic language with the said, calls for infinite interruption."[17] And that, "The saying calls for constant reflection in order to interrupt the said."[18] The saying exposes a work as "a site of fracture."[19] Or "The poem must interrupt in the name of the saying."[20] This is all to say that the *saying* is a site of rupture, a site of becoming, of beginning again and again. The *saying* is a site of the lyric "and." The *said*, in contrast, is static and closed and no longer participates in an engagement with language, with reader, with lyric self, etc. Revision, both in the sense of Schwitters' expansion, and in the sense of Ponge's renewal of perception, exists as an act of interruption. It is "Saying holding open its openness…Saying saying itself, without thematizing it, but exposing it again."[21] Think of Emily Dickinson's variants or Walt Whitman's "preoccupation with the subject of beginnings and the notion of origin…grounded in the notion of repetition."[22] These two authors/poets use revision to maintain their obsessive engagement with disruption of finalized meaning. Note that their revision exists as part of the presentation, not as something happening unseen and outside of the text. This is the kind of revision that remains open, that fractures the *said* by *saying*.

## Entryway VI:
## Performance Art & Alchemical Transformation

"To 'prove' an idea, for Montaigne, was to examine it in order to *find out* how true it was."[23]

About a month ago, a friend who recently completed training as a hypnotherapist came to visit me. While she was here, she performed an alchemical tarot reading for me using the Bruegel tarot deck. To conduct an alchemical tarot reading, you need to have a deck in which each card contains the image of a person. What makes the reading alchemical is that you choose a person in each card to identify with and then you take on their position in the card. By "take on," I mean that you physically enact their posture and expressions. Then you describe what it is like to be in this posture with this expression. The reading is alchemical because you conduct your own transformation. You are the reader of your own cards, facilitated by another witness. The "magic" in this kind of tarot reading is in the way it takes something invisible (a state of mind or body) and makes it visible (through posture and your verbalized interpretation of that posture). I've been thinking lately about how writing might allow or does allow simultaneous expression of the visible and the invisible, the conscious and the subconscious. Writing, or at least what I think of as good writing, hinges between these two things. Writing makes possible this intermediary state and creates a potential for metamorphosis.

I like the way that "metamorphosis" sounds like a parent word to "metaphor." It suggests that what metaphor is really about is transformation. Linguist Caitlin Walker discusses a language of inquiry that enables us to inquire, via metaphor, into our own experiences, somewhat like the alchemical tarot reading. She discusses psychotherapist David Grove's Five Clean Questions and how he applies them to fears and anxieties people are having in order for them to get to the metaphorical bottom of the issue, in order for them to engage a metamorphosis or transfiguration via language. Basically, what happens is that by getting one to discuss the location, attributes, sequence, and metaphors of a fear or anxiety, a narrative attaches to that fear or anxiety and uproots it from one's body.

My favorite performance artists, Ana Mendieta, Guillermo Gómez-Peña, and Cecilia Vicuña, engage this same kind of metaphor-metamorphosis. But they do so visually and at times the narrative may be less clear. What draws me to performance art is the engagement of alchemical interpretation. The possibility of giving it voice visually, linguistically, bodily. Performance art allows us to find out how true something is. It engages the articulation of gesture—gesticulation, what is becoming, what is being formed. It allows the self to inhabit many residences. It is a Merzbau for the lyric self, for any self. It is a poetry for the body. It whispers the word "and."

## Entryway VII: the Lyric And[24]

And here even dreams are like a network of tendons.
And the sky, an accident of stems.
And yes, we think the building looks like a road.
And this branch glues you home.
And I came out in its mouth like a dream of meat.
And then suddenly the parts come together again.
And in this I am—as Poetry is.
And are we gutted now or what.
And here is the steeple.
And there was the idea of thinking.
And above, the clouds stopped in motion.
And yet it turns.
And when we shake it, it looks like a new stranger.
And here we speak with voices.
And all our bodies caught apart.

# Notes

1   Marjorie Perloff, *Differentials: Poetry, Poetics, Pedagogy* (Tuscaloosa: U of Alabama Press, 2004), 67.

2   Giles Deleuze and Felix Guattari, *A Thousands Plateaus* (London: The Athlone Press, 2001), 27.

3   Alexander Smith, "On the Writing of Essays," in *Dreamthrop: a book of essays written in the country* (New York: E. P. Dutton & Co, 1912), accessed March 17, 2013, http://www.gutenberg.org/ebooks/18135. Quoted in Lopate, xliv.

4   Philip Lopate, *The Art of the Personal Essay* (New York: Anchor Books, 1997), xlii.

5   Theodor Adorno, "The Essay as Form," in *Notes to Literature*, vol. 1 (New York: Columbia UP, 1991). Quoted in Lopate, xliii.

6   William Zeiger, "The Exploratory Essay: Enfranchising the Spirit of Inquiry in College Composition," *College English* 47, no. 5 (1985), 455. Quoted in Lopate, xlv.

7   Mutlu Blasing, *Lyric Poetry: The Pain and Pleasure of Words* (Princeton: Princeton UP, 2009), 27-29.

8   Alex Preminger, Terry V.F. Brogan, and Frank J. Warnke, eds., *The New Princeton Encyclopedia of Poetry & Poetics* (Princeton: Princeton UP, 1993).

9   Qtd. in Ibid., 726.

10  Qtd. in ibid., 726.

11  Daniel Kane, *What Is Poetry: Conversations with the American Avant-Garde* (New York: Teachers & Writers Collaborative, 2003), 161.

12  Ibid., 161.

13  Ibid., 161.

**14** In 1923, Kurt Schwitters constructed a grotto-like surface consisting of collaged paper columns and sculptures that protruded from the walls and ceilings of his family home in Hanover, Germany.

**15** Madeline Gins and Arakawa, *Making Dying Illegal: Architecture Against Death: Original to the 21st Century* (New York: Roof Books, 2006).

**16** The Winchester House was continuously under construction by Sarah Winchester, widow to William Winchester of the Winchester Repeating Arms Company, for 38 years, from 1884-1922. Sarah believed the house was haunted by the spirits of those killed by the Winchester rifle and was told by a medium that she would be punished if she did not build ceaselessly. The odd layout, doors and stairways leading to nowhere, contributes to the haunted quality of the house.

**17** Qtd. in Colin Davis, *Levinas: An Introduction* (Notre Dame: U of Notre Dame Press, 1997) 75.

**18** Ibid., 78.

**19** Ibid., 164.

**20** Ibid., 166.

**21** Ibid., 78.

**22** Krystyna Mazur, *Poetry and Repetition.* (New York: Routledge, 2005) 39.

**23** Philip Lopate, *The Art of the Personal Essay* (New York: Anchor Books, 1997), xlv.

**24** Cento with lines from Suzanne Doppelt, Beverly Dahlen, Gennady Aygi, Oni Buchanan, Olivia Cronk, & Emily Pettit

• Aygi, Gennady. *Into the Snow.* Trans. Sarah Valentine. New York: Wave Books, 2011.

- Buchanan, Oni. *What Animal*. Athens: U of Georgia Press, 2003.
- Cronk, Olivia. *Skin Horse*. Notre Dame: Action Books, 2012.
- Dahlen, Beverly. *A Reading 18-20*. Boulder: Instance Press, 2006.
- Doppelt, Suzanne. *Ring Rang Wrong*. Trans. Cole Swensen. Providence: Burning Deck, 2004.
- Pettit, Emily. *Goat in the Snow*. Austin: Birds, LLC, 2012.

# LETTER MACHINE EDITIONS